Steam Memories: 1950's – 1960's

No. 48: THE STANIER JUBILEES

Pictures by **K Pirt, D Beecroft & D Dalton**

Copyright Book Law Publications 2012
ISBN 978-1-907094-27-9

INTRODUCTION

The Jubilee class of 4-6-0 were endowed with some of the most evocative names carried by any locomotive class on British Railways. Study the names in the *ABC* and it was out with the atlas just to see where those faraway places – those corners of the British Empire – were located. I have a theory which, as I've mentioned before, and so far been proven to be correct, that most train spotters excelled in geography at school, at least in the 50s and 60s! And that was usually because of certain locomotive classes such as the Jubilees. The other theory concerns history – British history of course, what other is there? – and, once again our young spotters usually excelled at school in that subject too. Why, well just study the other names carried by those Jubilees. Battles, leaders of all ranks, warships, winners and losers, names from history and all glorious! We wanted to know what each meant so, the natural fallout was knowledge. The LMS certainly knew how to celebrate the country which they served.

This album has been compiled to show various members of the class as they appeared in BR days. The illustrations show them in all guises – ex works condition, working express passenger, empty stock, goods and parcels trains, on shed, in decline. They are set out in numerical order but not all 191 members of the class are represented, just a good selection.

Cover Picture (see Page 4)

(previous page) **SILVER JUBILEE hauls a diverted Manchester (London Road)–London (Euston) express through Northwich in April 1959 during the period when electrification works south of Manchester were playing havoc with the schedules of express passenger trains, and other services, to and from London Road station. Although this engine had spent time at two of Manchester's depots, Newton Heath and latterly Longsight, at this time No.45552 was allocated to Edge Hill.** *D.H.Beecroft.*

Printed and bound by The Amadeus Press, Cleckheaton, West Yorkshire
First published in the United Kingdom by Book Law Publications, 382 Carlton Hill, Nottingham, NG4 1JA

The afternoon sun has enough light to show to advantage the stainless steel numbers 45552 attached to cab side of SILVER JUBILEE at Crewe North shed in August 1964. The date is getting late and this 'Jubilee' has acquired the cab warning stripe. Although once regarded as 'special' this member of the class was never afforded any special treatment by British Railways except, perhaps, the continuation of raised cab side numbers in 1951. If any celebrity status was ever given this engine, it no longer applied and its grotty external appearance was typical of this period. Note the de-named – ex ANZAC probably – and similarly scruffy 'Britannia' nosing into the picture on the right. *D.H.Beecroft.*

With No.45678 DE ROBECK alongside for company at Crewe North shed, No.45553 CANADA stables on one of the recently installed radial roads for the new roundhouse which was still in the making. The date is 15th March 1959 and AWS has begun to be made more widely available to BR after a manufacturing shortage. Being one of the WCML allocated express passenger engines, No.45553 has just had the equipment fitted. It was only eight months previously that this 'Jubilee' was finally coupled up to a Stanier 4000 gallon tender when No.10301, ex 8F No.48046, was attached during a Non-Classified repair at Rugby. Prior to that event in August 1958, No.45553 had hauled around Fowler type tenders since new. *K.R.Pirt.*

How they used to turn them out – No.45555 in the yard at Crewe works, March 1960. *D.H.Beecroft.*

No.45559 BRITISH COLUMBIA stands by the south wall of the paint shop at Crewe works in April 1954 after completing a Heavy Intermediate overhaul. Note the inside surfaces of the bogie wheels are painted too and, whilst your eyes are scanning that level of the illustration, look at the single wooden 'scotch' placed beneath the front of the leading coupled wheel! Based at Patricroft from May 1947 until November 1959, No.45559 was one of thirty-six 'Jubilees' which had been allocated at one time or another to Patricroft shed. Most had come and gone from 10C during the LMS period from February 1935 to the outbreak of war in 1939. During the war years a loyal half dozen worked from Patricroft, whilst post-war comings and goings brought a variety which kept the enthusiasts happy, if not the fitting staff. The last two active members were Nos.45593 which left for Newton Heath (and eventual preservation) in December 1964, and 45600 which followed to 26A but was condemned twelve months later. *K.R.Pirt.*

Leaving Rugby in its wake, No.45561 SASKATCHEWAN heads an Up Manchester (London Road)–London (Euston) express [W66] through the cutting at Clifton Road in August 1960. It wasn't usual to have a Kentish Town 'Jubilee' working Manchester-London expresses along the WCML but this particular 14B engine had just finished a Heavy General at Crewe and was making its way back to London whilst earning its keep! This 'Jubilee' had certainly been around during its twenty-six years to date – Bristol, Carlisle, Crewe, Liverpool, London, Manchester, Preston. Afterwards it would be allocated to the depots at Burton and then Derby from where it was withdrawn in September 1964. *D.H.Beecroft.*

No.45562 ALBERTA stables on one of the outside roads at Royston shed on 29th August 1966. It was most unusual to find a 'named' engine at this particular depot which, from its opening in 1932, dealt virtually exclusively with coal haulage from the surrounding coalfield therefore the allocation of freight locomotives reflected that fact. However, this was 1966 and all the old rules of 'what was used for what' seemed to vanish and it became the norm to use whatever was available – convention had gone out of the window. Note that all the other locomotives in frame are Stanier 8F 2-8-0s. *David Dalton.*

Having just three miles of its journey from Carlisle to Bradford to complete, No.45562 slows at the last intermediate station stop, the triangular junction station at Shipley, north of Bradford, with a southbound passenger working on 24th June 1967.

No.45562 is 'pegged' to continue its journey to Bradford (Forster Square). The line to the right is the route to Leeds, looking north-east.

Leaving Shipley behind and running across the junction onto the Leeds-Bradford line, No.45562 reveals its dirty left side to the camera. Nevertheless, No.45562 was to enjoy a type of celebrity status for the following three months as it covered for failed diesels and was specifically chosen for certain regular express passenger workings over the S&C, not to mention the odd railtour.

With two 'Royal Scots' for company, No.45564 NEW SOUTH WALES stands outside the paint shop at Crewe on Sunday 19th September 1954. Our subject had just finished a Casual Heavy overhaul and was released back into traffic the following day. For the record, its two companions were Nos.46123 and 46108. *David Dalton.*

Having been withdrawn during the previous January, No.45565 VICTORIA stands derelict and forlorn alongside the shed at Low Moor on 29th April 1967. Covered in grime and graffiti, the 'Jubilee' is missing a vital component in the shape of its chimney but the condemned engine will not need one any more. Note the painted backing plate standing in for its absent nameplate. *David Dalton.*

This is how No.45565 appeared in October 1964 when it was working a Bradford return excursion from Blackpool (Central) on a gloriously sunny though chilly afternoon. Immaculately turned out – cab stripe excepting – and complete with nameplates, No.45565 was at that time allocated to Low Moor shed (56F) and was intensively used for all sorts of traffic. Just over two years later it was condemned. *D.H.Beecroft.*

No.45570 NEW ZEALAND at Millhouses in March 1958. New to the 19B allocation in June 1957, this 'Jubilee' was around when the Eastern Region took over the former Midland depots in the Sheffield area. When Millhouses closed in 1962, this engine, along with others which had not transferred out of the area, moved over to Canklow. But, in June 1962, again with other ex 41C engines, it became part of the Darnall allocation but did little work, spending much of that year in store. Crewe had carried out a Heavy General overhaul on No.45570 during the final months of 1961 but it made little difference to the ER authorities who condemned the engine in December 1962. However, in this view taken some five years before that event, the 'Jubilee' looks magnificent with the early morning sun revealing much detail. Within a few weeks of this picture being recorded, NEW ZEALAND would be off to Crewe for a Heavy Intermediate, to be back at Millhouses in time to work the summer traffic of 1958. *K.R.Pirt.*

The soft morning sun reflects off Barrow Road's No.45572 EIRE at Millhouses in May 1958. Pre-war, this engine had been allocated to both of the Sheffield depots, Grimesthorpe for a couple of weeks in September 1937, and Millhouses for nearly eighteen months thereafter until moving to Trafford Park in early 1939. It remained at the Manchester depot throughout the duration of the war and right up to the eve of nationalisation when it transferred to Barrow Road. It was at Trafford Park where one of the lowest annual mileages for the class was recorded – in 1946, with no prolonged works visits to fall back on; No.5572 managed just 21,976 miles in revenue service. This was quite a change from the 64,820 miles run in 1940. The Bristol shed, by the very nature of its geographical position within the BR network in relation to the LM Region, could ensure high mileage for all of its 'Jubilees' No.45572 included. In 1958 a respectable 63,176 miles was recorded for EIRE. *K.R.Pirt.*

With bits and pieces removed, a dreadful looking No.45574 reposes on a dead-end siding at Holbeck shed in May 1966, some two months after withdrawal. Unlike some of the other Leeds 'Jubilees' which, towards the end had something of a cult following amongst enthusiasts, INDIA was allowed to remain in the same grimy state in which it arrived from Kingmoor in June 1965; its mechanical condition would certainly have had some bearing as to its future, long or short. *Chris Dunn.*

With eleven bogies in tow, No.45575 MADRAS runs into the outskirts of Sheffield past Dore & Totley South Junction in the summer of July 1956 heading a Down express. *K.R.Pirt.*

A nice atmospheric view of No.45585 HYDERABAD (Newton Heath), being double-headed by Class 5 No.45297 (Preston), out of Preston station in July 1961 with a Birmingham-Blackpool excursion. This was the steam railway. A recent acquisition by 26A, No.45585 was actually on summer loan from Leicester – yes they had some too – for work such as this. The summer of 1961 was still a busy time for depots such as Newton Heath. With package holidays abroad still in their infancy, certain depots had to borrow sometimes dozens of extra suitable engines from any shed they could to handle the holiday extras and daily excursions which were still popular with the public in general. For the record, and besides No.45585, Newton Heath borrowed the following off Leicester during that summer: Nos.45615, 45636, and 45650. *D.H.Beecroft.*

Relegated to freight duties by now, Crewe South 'Jubilee' No.45586 MYSORE sets out from Carlisle with a southbound working via the WCML in July 1964. This fascinating view of the junction south of Citadel passenger station shows the WCML in the background, complete with northbound passenger train, passing over the goods line whilst the double track nearer the camera carried goods trains from the former LNWR Crown Street goods station, situated in the right background, to Upperby junction, the point at which our subject joins the main line. Just above the 'Jubilee' are two further routes, the nearer being the former North Eastern line from Rome Street junction to London Road junction. The lines beyond that, just discernible to the left of the smoke, connected the Midland and NER main lines with Citadel station. After spending most of its life coupled with Fowler tenders, No.45586 was finally mated with a Stanier type in December 1959 – Mk.2 welded No.10742, ex Stanier 8F. Condemned in January 1965, MYSORE was sold for scrap to Cashmore's at Great Bridge. *D.H.Beecroft.*

No.45593 KOLHAPUR, newly acquired by Patricroft shed, makes an appearance at Blackpool in October 1964 just before Central shed was abandoned and Central passenger station was closed. This engine was a regular visitor at Blackpool during that last month of the 1964 illuminations traffic but besides working numerous excursions, No.45593 was also involved with the regular passenger services from Manchester too. After a three month residency at Newton Heath in early 1965, KOLHAPUR transferred to Holbeck in April 1965 for a two-year swansong after which preservation beckoned. *D.H.Beecroft.*

A nice three-quarter rear aspect of the recently double-chimney equipped No.45596 BAHAMAS as she steams through Stafford on Saturday 9th June 1962 with the northbound working of an enthusiasts special. This view of the junctions at the north end of Stafford station shows the four-track WCML heading towards Crewe whilst the branch to Wellington diverges to the left past the Bagnall factory. The line going off to the right was the former Great Northern route to Derby and points eastward – Stafford being the western limit of the East Coast company's territory. Note that the masts for the forthcoming WCML electrification are already fixed but completion of the catenary and associated wiring would not be until some time in the future. *David Dalton.*

In October 1963 No.45596 BAHAMAS had 'been in the wars' or to be more precise, its tender had. This view captured on Sunday 13th October at Horwich locomotive works, shows the working face of the tender but out of sight are the wagons carrying the two pieces – body and frames – of the tender (No.9045) after an accident at Farnley Junction earlier in the year. The event caused No.45596 to be condemned (there was nothing wrong with the engine) at Horwich but intervention by the Edgeley Shedmaster, Mr T.R.Smith, who persuaded Horwich to release his favoured BAHAMAS back to his custody with a 'makeshift' tender (No.10750). Of course we all know what occurred afterwards but it is worth noting that the intervention by one BR official certainly saved the day for No.45596 which went back into traffic prior to withdrawal in July 1966 and then preservation. *David Dalton.*

In the days when it was coupled to a Fowler tender (No.3939), No.45597 BARBADOS has charge of *THE THAMES CLYDE EXPRESS* as it enters the cutting at the south end of Dore & Totley station in July 1956. Having coupled onto the southbound express at Leeds, the Holbeck based 'Jubilee' has twelve bogies in tow but still has the easier stretch of the four-hundred plus miles journey of this long-lived named train. Note the small version of the BR emblem on the tender. *K.R.Pirt.*

When No.45597 arrived in Hull to await entry to Draper's scrapyard, it was bereft its outside, left hand cylinder although the coupling rod was still attached to the big 6ft 9in. diameter coupled wheels. Here the 4-6-0 is stabled in the fan of sidings known locally as '7 Section' alongside Dairycoates engine shed. Latterly allocated (actually since March 1940) to Leeds Holbeck shed, this was one of fourteen 'Jubilees' broken up by Draper's. For the record, the other thirteen were 45565, 45568, 45574, 45581, 45602, 45653, 45658, 45660, 45661, 45664, 45674, 45694, and 45739. *Chris Dunn.*

In February 1954, No.45598 BASUTOLAND awaits haulage away from Crewe works after completing a Light Intermediate overhaul – 29th December 1953 to 6th February 1954. Note the rather small BR lion and wheel emblem adorning the tender side; a tender change at its next 'General' in March 1955 would see one of the larger versions of the emblem applied, albeit to yet another Fowler tender. Allocated to Kentish Town since October 1946, this Jubilee had spent most of its life allocated to sheds on the old LMS Midland Division. Regaining a Stanier tender in November 1960, after nearly a quarter century coupled to the Fowler versions, No.45598 was sent, along with seventeen others of the class, to Burton-on-Trent some twelve months later to work off its remaining three years of life. *K.R.Pirt.*

No.45604 CEYLON at Crewe North shed 15th March 1959. Note the little touches of paint applied to the numberplate, and the securing bolts holding the smokebox fastening handles. *K.R.Pirt.*

Making a station stop at Stafford during the latter part of March 1959, No.45604 heads a Down empty stock train from the Birmingham direction. This is a nice view of the west side of Stafford station before the massive rebuilding and re-alignment which altered the overall appearance of this station considerably. *K.R.Pirt.*

With an acknowledgement from the crew to photographer Keith Pirt, No.45604 CEYLON makes a rapid start away from Stafford with its lightweight load. This engine transferred away from Crewe in May 1962 going to Carnforth, a shed not normally associated with 'Jubilees', other than visitors. After a year in north Lancashire No.45604 moved on to Kingmoor but was back at Carnforth by the end of the summer timetable. A year later Warrington Dallam, yet another establishment with little history of caring for 'Jubilees' became the home shed for CEYLON. Finally, in April 1965 and after nearly five months in storage, Newton Heath beckoned but in the following July the inevitable took place and No.45604 was consigned to scrap. *K.R.Pirt.*

An undated view of No.45608 GIBRALTAR, in charge of a northbound e.c.s. working, at Nottingham (Victoria). The Holbeck based 'Jubilee' has halted in the Down Slow No.2 awaiting signals whilst locally based K3 No.61943, heading a Down fitted goods, occupies the Down Goods line, alongside. The comparison in smokebox diameters is readily apparent with the Gresley engine looking very much like a character from *Thomas the Tank*. The fate of this particular 'Jubilee' along with sister No.45573, was to end up at the Clayton & Davie scrapyard on Tyneside; pictures of both appear in another album from this series, No.19 *North East Scrapyards*, David Dunn 2008. The same album contains illustrations of two other 'Jubilees, Nos.45584 and 45736 in a yard at North Blyth. *D.H.Beecroft.*

On a bright Sunday morning, 13th February 1955, No.45609 GILBERT AND ELLICE ISLANDS presents a near broadside view whilst stabled in the crowded yard at Millhouses shed. This engine carried one of the larger nameplates worn by the class and was affixed at Crewe works during a Heavy General overhaul in September 1936 whilst allocated to Barrow Road shed. Except for the initial six months of its life, when it worked on the Western Division of the LMS, No.45609 spent the rest of its time working from sheds on the old Midland Division including Holbeck in the north, Bristol in the west and Kentish Town in the south. It was allocated to Millhouses in October 1942 when it spent just over a year working from 19B. It resided for another five months at the Sheffield shed in 1946 but in September 1950 moved back to Millhouses in a transfer that proved to be its last. No.45609 made history of sorts in September 1960 when it became the first 'Jubilee' to be withdrawn from causes other than accidental, although it had been involved some years earlier in an accident which could have proven fatal. One of the wartime allocations which remains something of a mystery was the 2nd March 1940 transfer of No.5609 from Kentish Town to Toton from where it worked until the following 18th May when it returned to London. The Fowler type tender (this example was No.4494) was a near permanent companion to this engine except during wartime when it was coupled to a Stanier Mk.2 welded type, No.9772 from November 1939 to September 1946. *K.R.Pirt.*

No.45618 NEW HEBRIDES appears to have been halfway through a thorough clean at Trafford Park shed when it was called upon to work a London turn. Here on 29th September 1955 the Manchester based 'Jubilee' rests at Kentish Town shed after working an express into St Pancras. Subsidence and uneven track work was more often than not associated with those depots and yards situated in the coalfields of the Midlands and the North, but look at the track beneath the cab and tender of our subject - the peak and gradients have opened a yawning gap between engine and tender. *David Dalton.*

No.45619 runs through Dore & Totley with a Down express in 1956. *K.R.Pirt.*

On the same Saturday in June 1962 that No.45596 was out working the enthusiasts special, No.45624 ST HELENA was on shed at Stafford having worked in from Nuneaton. *David Dalton.*

A rather dirty No.45627 SIERRA LEONE of Kentish Town, runs a St Pancras bound express round the curve at Dore & Totley in the autumn of 1955. The painted smokebox is a result of a visit to works for a Casual Light repair during September and October. For all the muck, No.45627 managed to clock up a decent mileage of 72,000 that year, besides spending nine weeks out of traffic at main works. Fortunate enough to receive a Heavy General in March 1962, SIERRA LEONE lasted in traffic until September 1966 working from Bank Hall shed although between September 1962 and April 1966 it did spend five periods, some quite lengthy, in serviceable storage. *K.R.Pirt.*

Some eight years later No.45627 was still sporting a coat of filth when it was photographed outside Blackpool's Central shed on a sunny Saturday afternoon in October 1964. By now the 4-6-0 was based at Bank Hall and had worked into Blackpool on illuminations excursion 1T85. The diagonal stripe on the cabside had restricted its movements somewhat although the chances of SIERRA LEONE working under the wires south of Crewe were very slim anyway, the last time it was allocated to a Western Division shed was during the early years of WWII when it was at Crewe North, since which time it had been working from Midland Division sheds and latterly from the former Central Division shed at Liverpool. Note the deserted interior of Central shed which was about to close. The motor coaches over the fence to the right had won the day! *D.H.Beecroft.*

A diverted WCML freight heads through Whalley, with Upperby's No.45632 TONGA at the head, on Saturday 24th February 1962. Only the first five wagons appear to be fitted; a 5-plank open, merchandise, two Conflats with containers, another 5-plank open, then a pair of 12-ton ventilated vans of which only the first appears to be fitted. Note the tarpaulin on the nearest container protecting the contents from a leaking roof! *David Dalton.*

Blowing off with a definite roar, No.45633 ADEN has just emerged from beneath the coaling plant at Preston shed on Monday afternoon, 14th April 1958. After ten years allocated to Preston shed, No.45633 was transferred to Carnforth shed in September 1961 after the closure of Preston depot. From thereon it was downhill all the way with a stint at Derby from March to July 1963 then finally a move to Warrington Dallam where suitable work was difficult to come by. Although it was as late as October 1965 before this 'Jubilee' was condemned, for much of 1964 and all of 1965 it was in storage. *K.R.Pirt.*

Kentish Town's No.45641 SANDWICH basks in the morning sun at Trafford Park shed on Saturday 18th June 1955. The reason for the cleanliness of the locomotive – neither Kentish Town nor Trafford Park were renowned for there engine cleaning – can be explained away by the fact that No.45641 had just completed a Heavy General overhaul at Crewe (14th March to 23rd April) and some of the glint applied then still clings to the 'Jubilee' beneath the first micro coat of dust. Being allocated to 14B made this a high mileage engine and in 1955 it covered over 60,000 miles which although respectable seems 'average' compared to the three year period 1936, 1937 and 1938 when Kentish Town achieved 73,105, 72,213, and 78,288 miles respectively with No.5641, inclusive of seventeen weeks in main works during that time (in 1935 Preston, Barrow Road and Crewe sheds managed to get 72,961 miles out of it at the start of its life). Post-war, mileage's for the 'Jubilees' was somewhat lower than those attained pre-war but some depots, Kentish Town amongst them, still managed 60,000 plus miles per annum from their engines. *K.R.Pirt.*

Stabled at the home of the WDs in Wakefield, Farnley Junction based No.45643, formerly RODNEY, looks no better kept externally than the Austerity 2-8-0s surrounding it in this April 1965 view. The 4-6-0 later transferred to Holbeck in September but was laid-up shortly after the Christmas traffic peak and withdrawn a few weeks later in January 1966. Built at Crewe in December 1934, nearly three years were to pass before this engine was named, an event which occurred during a works visit in October 1937. During that time no fewer than five depots had used its services, including Aberdeen Ferryhill where it was allocated at the time of naming. It was during its three years and five months residency at Aberdeen when this 'Jubilee' attained its highest recorded annual mileage – 77,381 in 1936! *Chris Dunn.*

In better times, No.45643 goes through the final days of a Light Intermediate repair at Crewe on 3rd November 1957. *David Dalton.*

No.45647 STURDEE stands clean, marked-up and ready for entry to the Erecting shop at Crewe for a major overhaul in April 1964. Nearly thirty years earlier, at the end of the 1935 summer timetable when just over half of the class had been delivered, and before they started to receive those famous names, the distribution of those delivered (5552–5664) was as follows: Camden 17, Crewe North 27 (not a true reflection of the allocation at 5A as all those engines delivered new to the LMS went firstly to Crewe North for acceptance and running-in.), Derby 5, Durran Hill 1, Edge Hill 1, Grimesthorpe 2, Holbeck 14, Kentish Town 14, Newton Heath 1, Nottingham 3, Preston 11, Rugby 4, Upperby 9, Willesden 3. Nine years later on the eve of D-Day when Britain's war machine was probably as its most productive, the distribution of the 'Jubilee' class was: Barrow Road 8, Blackpool 7, Camden 13, Crewe North 21, Corkerhill 8, Derby 8, Edge Hill 9, Farnley Junction 5, Grimesthorpe 2, Holbeck 22, Kentish Town 12, Kingmoor 15, Longsight 17, Millhouses 10, Newton Heath 12, Polmadie 4, Saltley 1, Trafford Park 5, Upperby 12. The only real surprise amongst the class at that time was perhaps the singleton at Saltley (5626) and a pair still at Grimesthorpe (now 5652 and 5665, previously 5630 and 5649). *D.H.Beecroft.*

Not quite ready for the 'off' with a southbound express, No.45651 SHOVELL has its tender replenished from the water column on platform 6 at Sheffield (Midland) in 1956. A Bristol Barrow Road engine (January 1953 to September 1961), it had previously been allocated to Holbeck so was no stranger to this route. This wonderful period view shows the housing which once towered above the east side of Midland station, note also the partly demolished overall arched roof over platforms 7 to 9. *K.R.Pirt.*

After a Light Intermediate overhaul, No.45655 KEITH is brought back into daylight outside the Erecting shop at Crewe in March 1960. AWS was fitted during this visit but only the necessary hole had been drilled in the frame beneath the cab side sheet; it looks like a job for the outside gang. A certain amount of painting, mainly a priming coat, would also be carried out prior to a visit to the paint shop. *D.H.Beecroft.*

No.45656 COCHRANE appears to be in trouble as it struggles to a halt alongside Millhouses Park with an Up morning express in early June 1955. With steam seemingly issuing from the direction of the rear of the middle cylinder, the disgraced Millhouses 'Jubilee' was uncoupled from the train and replaced by Stanier Class 5 No.45447 of Kentish Town shed which then took the 'express' onto St Pancras. The proximity of 19B shed obviously speeded up the changeover. *K.R.Pirt.*

No.45656 in trouble again! It is now May 1959 and although still a Millhouses engine, it is languishing on the yard at Nottingham shed having had the centre set of coupled wheels removed. The reason for the 4-2-2 configuration is unknown as is the length of time COCHRANE was laid up at Nottingham awaiting repair. Neither the History Card nor local documents give any hint of what the problem might have been. Admitted, many locomotives attended the depots which had either wheel-drops or lifting shear legs as a matter of course but No.45656 would have more than likely visited Grimesthorpe shed, or even Darnall if the axle, wheels, or whatever it was, required attention. This could well have been a case of the 'Jubilee' working a northbound express through Nottingham and coming to grief whilst in the area. 16A would then have been the obvious port of call, even if being towed. However, look at the coal in the tender; besides being 'a nice drop of stuff' there is also rather a lot of it. It is as though our subject was whisked beneath the Nottingham coaler prior to having the defect looked at! Also, the presence of the BR emblem on the tender at this late date seems curious as this locomotive had attended Crewe for two Heavy Intermediate overhauls since the introduction of the BR crest. No.45656 eventually returned to Millhouses shed and normal traffic but was one of those 41C engines sent firstly to Canklow and then Darnall for the inevitable periods of storage when Millhouses closed in January 1962. In December 1962 this engine joined the other forty members of the class withdrawn during that year. *D.H.Beecroft.*

With apparent steam to spare, No.45659 DRAKE rushes a Down express through Wellingborough in 1956. The Midland main line and its various branches from St Pancras to Leeds via Nottingham, Derby, and Sheffield was the ideal route for these 6Ps; nothing too strenuous, medium weight trains, and lots of four-track sections where overtaking could be carried out with relative ease! The concentration of the class at former Midland Railway depots during the first ten years of BR's existence saw a fairly consistent number of engines working the express passenger traffic from seven depots. The engine sheds at Bristol, Derby, Kentish Town, Leeds, Millhouses, Nottingham and Trafford Park had just over a third of the class allocated at any one time with aggregate numbers totalling in the low 70s. The final year of the decade, 1959, saw numbers fall slightly as Trafford Park lost all but one of its usual six or seven 'Jubilees' in favour of half a dozen 'Britannia' Pacifics but the other sheds kept hold of their lot until dieselisation took hold. *David Dalton.*

Further evidence of the unusual circumstances prevailing towards the end of steam on BR is highlighted here at Kirkby-in-Ashfield engine shed in May 1965 when No.45660 ROOKE spent the weekend amongst the depot's 8F motive power. What traffic brought this Holbeck 'Jubilee' to the East Midlands freight depot is unknown but basically it could have been anything from haulage of empty mineral wagons to a parcels or goods working into nearby Mansfield. Within days No.45660 was back on the main line north of Leeds, sharing the Anglo-Scottish passenger trains with the diesels. One year after its visit to Kirkby, ROOKE was condemned. *D.H.Beecroft.*

A splendid looking No.45663 JERVIS rests on Millhouses shed in December 1954, ready to work back home. This Bristol Barrow Road based engine was one of a dozen 'Jubilees' allocated to 22A at that time, the others being 45561, 45572, 45577, 45602, 45651, 45660, 45662, 45682, 45685, 45690, 45699. The Bristol engines tended to put in some good annual mileage's with JERVIS achieving 68,023 miles in 1954 whilst in 1956, even though attending works at Crewe for a Heavy General overhaul during the summer, it attained nearly 72,000 miles! In September 1961 Barrow Road lost many of its 'Jubilees' to Shrewsbury (No.45663 had left in January 1958, transferring to Derby); only Nos.45682 TRAFALGAR, 45685 BARFLEUR, and 45690 LEANDER were kept on but by 1964 they too had been laid aside for withdrawal with '90' succumbing in March, '85' in April and finally '82' in June. *K.R.Pirt.*

Looking every bit a candidate for withdrawal, No.45670, formerly HOWARD OF EFFINGHAM, resides at Crewe South on 19th September 1964 – just a month away from condemnation! Woodford owned this engine during the summer of 1964 but, according to the record, it was soon to pass to Stockport Edgeley for a brief period prior to withdrawal. *David Dalton.*

No.45674 DUNCAN was a long-time resident of Crewe North (December 1941 to March 1963) and here on Sunday 23rd January 1955 it takes in the afternoon sun shortly after release from works. Three weeks in shops for a Light Intermediate overhaul was enough to keep No.45674 in traffic for another year before a Heavy General, complete with a change of boiler was required. Note that the paint brush has been used sparingly on this visit, the bufferbeam appearing to be the only part of the engine so treated but it was only a LI. Although Crewe North sent its 'Jubilees' far and wide over a variety of routes, none of the engines ran up large annual mileages and anything over 55,000 miles might have been deemed exceptional. No.45674 was no different to any other 5A 6P in that respect although it is recorded that during 1936 it clocked-up more than 85,000 miles – as a Preston engine! After going into store during September 1962 – a seemingly bad year for the class – it was transferred to Saltley in March 1963 to pay off some of the cost of a Heavy General overhaul carried out at the end of 1961. After eighteen months at 21A it was transferred back to Crewe North but never made the journey because it was condemned beforehand. *K.R.Pirt.*

In the summer of 1963 Saltley's newly acquired 'Jubilee' No.45674 DUNCAN departs from the Gloucester station stop and crosses Tramway Junction at Barnwood heading for Birmingham (New Street) whilst in charge of the Bristol–Birmingham leg of a cross-country, south-west to north-east express (1N84). *D.H.Beecroft.*

No.45676 CODRINGTON heads through Millhouses bound for London with a Sheffield (Midland) to St Pancras express in April 1954. It was unusual for a Camden based 'Jubilee' or indeed any 1B engine to work over the Midland main line so it must be assumed that Kentish Town had the engine on loan for a short period. *K.R.Pirt.*

No.45679 ARMADA was smitten with a Fowler tender in 1937 just eighteen months after coming into traffic with a new 4000 gallon Stanier type which was given to a 'Royal Scot'. Here on a cold 24th February 1962, the Newton Heath engine runs north-east over the Whalley loop with a diverted WCML express. *David Dalton.*

54

45682 TRAFALGAR bathes in the morning sun at Millhouses shed in 1956. Another Barrow Road engine, No.45682 is turned, coaled and ready for working home later in the day. *K.R.Pirt.*

Tucked out of the way at the west side of the shed, No.45683 HOGUE spends a weekend at its home depot, Millhouses, in January 1955. Although not evident, the 4-6-0 had spent most of the previous month at Crewe works undergoing a Light Intermediate overhaul which would keep it in good stead before its next 'General' in late 1956. Transferred officially to Millhouses on the last day of the LMS, No.45683 remained at the Sheffield shed until its closure in 1962 after which the 6P was sent to nearby Canklow then to the former LNER depot at Darnall. HOGUE'S withdrawal in December 1962 was not surprising as many of the ex Millhouses engines had ended up at Darnall where they spent much of the time in store. *K.R.Pirt.*

Barrow Road based No.45685 BARFLEUR rushes through Millhouses with a West of England express in April 1954. Like most of the Bristol engines, No.45685 put in some hefty annual mileages compared with the rest of the class but the 54,341 miles achieved in 1954 did not turn out to be one of its vintage years – perhaps two months attending works had some bearing on the total. However, this 'Jubilee' attained the highest ever annual mileage for the class when in 1938, and working from Kentish Town, it clocked up 93,588 miles. It also spent more than five weeks at main works undergoing its first 'Heavy General'. *K.R.Pirt.*

Carrying the obligatory large cab side numbers applied at St Rollox works, No.45687 NEPTUNE heads a line of assorted stabled locomotives at Corkerhill engine shed on Saturday 25th May 1957. The 6P had arrived at 67A in September 1952 from Upperby and was accompanied by Nos.45621, 45665, 45687, 45711 and 45720 from other English depots. Besides those 'Jubilees' which came north to Corkerhill that month from the London Midland Region, a similar number were transferred south away from Corkerhill and the Scottish Region to depots in England: Nos.45560, 45576, 45643, 45645, and 45646. During that same period in 1952 an even larger number of locomotives, some thirty or so, were involved in a mass swap between four ScR depots and a dozen or so LM sheds. The reason for the transfers is unknown but enthusiasts on both sides of the border would have been no doubt pleased after their initial puzzlement. With that little exercise out of the way, Corkerhill's compliment of 'Jubilees' amounted to some half dozen which were kept throughout the Fifties' and into the next decade. During the early months of 1960 another batch arrived at 67A from various sheds to bring the depot's allocation up to eleven. However, all good things must pass and by June 1962 many of those engines were stored unserviceable at either Corkerhill or at another storage site established some distance away at Lugton. Amongst those at the latter place were Nos.45621, 45665, 45707, 45711 and 45720. Keeping them company were two 2P 4-4-0s, Nos.40620 and 40621, and a solitary 'Duchess' No.46227. By September all of the 67A 'Jubs' were laid up ready for the mass cull which took place in December as all of Corkerhill's 6Ps were condemned and consigned for scrap. Those involved being: Nos.45621, 45665, 45673, 45677, 45687, 45692, 45693, 45707, 45711, 45720, and 45727! For the record the two 'Scots' which had transferred to Corkerhill from Polmadie, Nos.46102 and 46104, were also condemned. *David Dalton.*

No.45687 enters Stranraer on Sunday 15th July 1962 with a passenger working from Glasgow. Within weeks this engine was laid-up awaiting the inevitable. *David Dalton.*

No.45689 AJAX, fresh out of the paint shop, stands in the yard at Crewe works on Sunday 23rd January 1955. This short-named 'Jubilee' had just undergone a Heavy General overhaul which was started on 13th December 1954 but was not completed until 13th February 1955, some three weeks after this portrait was captured on film. Obviously the Longsight based engine must have fallen victim to some anomalies which revealed themselves after this excellent paint job was completed; but we shall never know what. The Mark 1 riveted tender, No.9160, was coupled to AJAX throughout its life, a not unusual occurrence within the 'Jubilee' class. *K.R.Pirt.*

Surrounded by a nice array of semaphore signals, locally based No.45692 CYCLOPS approaches Perth from the south with the Euston–Perth express. Transferred to Perth in August 1954 from Polmadie, this engine had been allocated to English sheds up to January 1941. In May 1960 it moved back south but only as far as Corkerhill where, in December 1962, it was condemned. The tender of sister No.45697 is just discernible on the left. *D.H.Beecroft.*

Unlined and certainly unnamed, No.45697 on 29th April 1967 'somewhere in West Yorkshire' with a lined but black painted tender from an unknown Stanier Class 5. The swap enabled this Holbeck engine to work until September 1967 and be amongst the last three active members of the class. *David Dalton*.

In the days before it acquired a Stanier tender, and when it also carried nameplates, No.45697 ACHILLES is seen in May 1959 passing the motive power depot as it enters Perth with a parcels train from Carlisle. In July 1964, whilst attending Crewe for overhaul and by then allocated to Farnley Junction, the last of the various Fowler tenders coupled to this engine throughout its life up to that date, was exchanged for one of the larger 4,000 gallon Stanier types; that example must have been in questionable health because within a few years ACHILLES had to acquire yet another tender as evidenced by the last but one illustration. *D.H.Beecroft.*

63

Barrow Road's No.45699 GALATEA simmers in platform 2 at Gloucester (Eastgate) with the Paignton-Bradford *DEVONIAN* in the spring of 1957. The Driver and Fireman are already out on the platform preparing to put the bag in as an observer looks on. The route of this named train, and other cross-country north-east to south-west workings ensured a number of station stops en route compared with other express passenger trains between say the capital and the provincial cities. Ending up at Shrewsbury in 1961, GALATEA was withdrawn in November 1964 but was spared the short journey to Crewe for cutting up because that works had by then curtailed the scrapping of steam locomotives, relying instead on the private contractors to dismantle BR's remaining fleet of steam locomotives. In that respect No.45699 was lucky in being sold to a yard in Barry and the rest, of course, is history. *David Dalton*.

Trafford Park's No.45705 SEAHORSE holds its own amongst the diesels on Derby shed yard in March 1965. Note the nameplate still in situ at this late date. Spending the first twenty years of its life at Farnley Junction shed, No.45705, like the other Farnley 'Jubilees,' clocked-up only moderate mileage's compared with their sister engines allocated down the road at Holbeck. Farnley's lot would average mid to high 30 thousand mile annual averages whilst Holbeck's gang could each knock-up an average in the high 50 and low 60 thousand mile brackets. *Chris Dunn.*

No.45702 COLOSSUS runs into the south end of Preston station in July 1961 with a less than taxing, one vehicle parcels train. This engine started and ended its life at Newton Heath but during the period June 1938 to December 1950 it was transferred a number of times to five other sheds, not including a five year stint at 26A from October 1938. The shiny bit of paintwork on the cylinder stems from a recent visit to Crewe for a Casual Light repair. Note that AWS was yet to be fitted in a job carried out during the following December. *D.H.Beecroft.*

Newton Heath's No.45710 IRRESISTIBLE spent most of its life working from the former Central Division sheds – Central Division of the LMS, the former Lancashire & Yorkshire Railway – chiefly Newton Heath. However, the Manchester (Victoria)–Glasgow (Central) expresses regularly brought the Manchester based 'Jubilees' to Glasgow and in May 1959 No.45710 is all ready to work back home after being serviced at Polmadie shed. Another 'Jubilee' albeit unidentified, has joined the line of stabled engines ready to work southbound trains. *D.H.Beecroft.*

Another Central Division 'Jubilee' No.45719 GLORIOUS of Bank Hall, graces the yard at Polmadie shed in May 1959. After running coupled to Fowler type tenders for the much of its life, this 'Jubilee' was finally married up to one of the larger 4000 gallon Stanier tenders during a Heavy Intermediate overhaul in November 1958. *D.H.Beecroft.*

No.45720 INDOMITABLE at Corkerhill in May 1959 with a Sou'-Western lines semaphore indicator attached to the upper lamp iron. This was one of the engines which came from the LMR in September 1952 when a similar number of 'Jubilees' were swapped between Scottish Region and LM Region. Shortly after this picture was taken, No.45720 transferred to Perth but returned to 67A in April 1960 via Polmadie. It was another victim of the December 1962 cull. *D.H.Beecroft.*

With a WD 2-8-0, a Caley 0-6-0 and a Class 5 for company, Perth based No.45727 INFLEXIBLE settles at St Rollox shed in April 1959. Sister engines Nos.45728 to 45732 spent much of their lives working from sheds either in Scotland or, in the case of Kingmoor, in the Scottish Region and were inevitably overhauled at St Rollox works. The latter engines transferred south to Lancashire during 1961 or 62, whilst No.45727 became a victim of the Corkerhill cull in December 1962. *D.H.Beecroft.*

Rebuilt No.45735 COMET runs through the cutting at Clifton Road, south of Rugby with a late morning Wolverhampton-Euston express (W296) in August 1960. A Preston engine at this time, COMET was looking the worse for wear externally though it appears steam tight at least. This was the 7P 'Jubilee' which ended up at Annesley shed working the Nottingham (Victoria)–London (Marylebone) expresses over the Great Central route from late 1963 to withdrawal in October 1964. 6P No.45626 had preceded it to the Nottinghamshire depot by a year, along with a dozen or so 'Royal Scots' but had left Annesley three months later for Burton. *D.H.Beecroft*

Sister 7P 'Jubilee' No.45736 PHOENIX appears to be in much better condition in June 1961 as it runs through Nuneaton (Trent Valley) with an Up Manchester-Euston express [W576]. The Crewe North engine was just ex-works after a Heavy General overhaul – 19th April to 26th May – when the speedometer was fitted. Both of the 'Rebuilt Jubilees' had been worked-on to upgrade them during the early months of 1942! Some might query the rebuilding as extravagant during a period of WW2 when materials and indeed personnel were required for more pressing causes. Nevertheless, these two remained as the only 'Jubilees' so treated. No.45736 was withdrawn a month prior to No.45735's demise. *D.H.Beecroft.*